Francis Frith's

THE CORNISH COAST

PHOTOGRAPHIC MEMORIES

Francis Frith's

THE CORNISH COAST

◆

Martin Dunning

First published in the United Kingdom in hardback in 2000
by The Francis Frith Collection®

Hardback edition
ISBN 1-85937-163-9

Paperback edition published 2003
ISBN 1-85937-495-6

Reprinted in paperback 2004, 2006

Text and Design copyright The Francis Frith Collection®
Photographs copyright The Francis Frith Collection®
except where indicated.

The Frith® photographs and the Frith® logo are reproduced under
licence from Heritage Photographic Resources Ltd,
the owners of the Frith® archive and trademarks.
'The Francis Frith Collection', 'Francis Frith' and 'Frith' are
registered trademarks of Heritage Photographic Resources Ltd.

British Library Cataloguing in Publication Data

The Cornish Coast Photographic Memories
Martin Dunning
ISBN 1-85937-495-6

The Francis Frith Collection
Frith's Barn, Teffont,
Salisbury, Wiltshire SP3 5QP
Tel: +44 (0) 1722 716 376
Email: info@francisfrith.co.uk
www.francisfrith.com

Printed and bound in Great Britain

Front Cover: MOUSEHOLE *1927* 79949t

*The colour-tinting is for illustrative purposes only, and is not intended
to be historically accurate*

Every attempt has been made to contact copyright holders of
illustrative material. We will be happy to give full acknowledgement
in future editions for any items not credited. Any information
should be directed to The Francis Frith Collection.

AS WITH ANY HISTORICAL DATABASE THE FRITH ARCHIVE IS
CONSTANTLY BEING CORRECTED AND IMPROVED AND THE
PUBLISHERS WOULD WELCOME INFORMATION ON OMISSIONS
OR INACCURACIES

CONTENTS

FRANCIS FRITH
VICTORIAN PIONEER

FRANCIS FRITH, founder of the world-famous photographic archive, was a complex and multi-talented man. A devout Quaker and a highly successful Victorian businessman, he was philosophical by nature and pioneering in outlook.

By 1855 he had already established a wholesale grocery business in Liverpool, and sold it for the astonishing sum of £200,000, which is the equivalent today of over £15,000,000. Now a very rich man, he was able to indulge his passion for travel. As a child he had pored over travel books written by early explorers, and his fancy and imagination had been stirred by family holidays to the sublime mountain regions of Wales and Scotland. 'What lands of spirit-stirring and enriching scenes and places!' he had written. He was to return to these scenes of grandeur in later years to 'recapture the thousands of vivid and tender memories', but with a different purpose. Now in his thirties, and captivated by the new science of photography, Frith set out on a series of pioneering journeys up the Nile and to the Near East that occupied him from 1856 until 1860.

INTRIGUE AND EXPLORATION

These far-flung journeys were packed with intrigue and adventure. In his life story, written when he was sixty-three, Frith tells of being held captive by bandits, and of fighting 'an awful midnight battle to the very point of surrender with a deadly pack of hungry, wild dogs'. Wearing flowing Arab costume, Frith arrived at Akaba by camel sixty years before Lawrence of Arabia, where he encountered 'desert princes and rival sheikhs, blazing with jewel-hilted swords'.

He was the first photographer to venture beyond the sixth cataract of the Nile. Africa was still the mysterious 'Dark Continent', and Stanley and Livingstone's historic meeting was a decade into the future. The conditions for picture taking confound belief. He laboured for hours in his wicker dark-room in the sweltering heat of the desert, while the volatile chemicals fizzed dangerously in their trays. Back in London he exhibited his photographs and was 'rapturously cheered' by members of the Royal Society. His reputation as a photographer was made overnight.

VENTURE OF A LIFE-TIME

Characteristically, Frith quickly spotted the opportunity to create a new business as a specialist publisher of photographs. He lived in an era of immense and sometimes violent change.

For the poor in the early part of Victoria's reign work was exhausting and the hours long, and people had precious little free time to enjoy themselves. Most had no transport other than a cart or gig at their disposal, and rarely travelled far beyond the boundaries of their own town or village. However, by the 1870s the railways had threaded their way across the country, and Bank Holidays and half-day Saturdays had been made obligatory by Act of Parliament. All of a sudden the working man and his family were able to enjoy days out and see a little more of the world.

With typical business acumen, Francis Frith foresaw that these new tourists would enjoy having souvenirs to commemorate their days out. In 1860 he married Mary Ann Rosling and set out on a new career: his aim was to photograph every city, town and village in Britain. For the next thirty years he travelled the country by train and by pony and trap, producing fine photographs of seaside resorts and beauty spots that were keenly bought by millions of Victorians. These prints were painstakingly pasted into family albums and pored over during the dark nights of winter, rekindling precious memories of summer excursions.

THE RISE OF FRITH & CO

Frith's studio was soon supplying retail shops all over the country. To meet the demand he gathered about him a small team of photographers, and published the work of independent artist-photographers of the calibre of Roger Fenton and Francis Bedford. In order to gain some understanding of the scale of Frith's business one only has to look at the catalogue issued by Frith & Co in 1886: it runs to some 670 pages, listing not only many thousands of views of the British Isles but also many photographs of most European countries, and China, Japan, the USA and Canada - note the sample page shown on page 9 from the hand-written Frith & Co ledgers recording the pictures. By 1890 Frith had created the greatest specialist photographic publishing company in the world, with over 2,000 sales outlets - more than the combined number that Boots and WH Smith have today! The picture on the next page shows the Frith & Co display board at Ingleton in the Yorkshire Dales (left of window). Beautifully constructed with a mahogany frame and gilt inserts, it could display up to a dozen local scenes.

POSTCARD BONANZA

The ever-popular holiday postcard we know today took many years to develop. In 1870 the Post Office issued the first plain cards, with a pre-printed stamp on one face. In 1894 they allowed other publishers' cards to be sent through the mail with an attached adhesive halfpenny stamp. Demand grew rapidly, and in 1895 a new size of postcard was permitted called the court card, but there was little room for illustration. In 1899, a year after Frith's death, a new card measuring 5.5 x 3.5 inches became the standard format, but it was not until 1902 that the divided back came into being, so that the address and message could be on one face and a full-size illustration on the other. Frith & Co were in the vanguard of postcard development: Frith's sons Eustace and Cyril continued their father's monumental task, expanding the number of views offered to the public and recording more and more places

in Britain, as the coasts and countryside were opened up to mass travel.

Francis Frith had died in 1898 at his villa in Cannes, his great project still growing. The archive he created continued in business for another seventy years. By 1970 it contained over a third of a million pictures showing 7,000 British towns and villages.

FRANCIS FRITH'S LEGACY

Frith's legacy to us today is of immense significance and value, for the magnificent archive of evocative photographs he created provides a unique record of change in the cities, towns and villages throughout Britain over a century and more. Frith and his fellow studio photographers revisited locations many times down the years to update their views, compiling for us an enthralling and colourful pageant of British life and character.

We are fortunate that Frith was dedicated to recording the minutiae of everyday life, for it is this sheer wealth of visual data, the painstaking chronicle of changes in dress, transport, street layouts, buildings, housing, engineering and landscape that captivates us so much today. His remarkable images offer us a powerful link with the past and with the lives of our ancestors.

THE VALUE OF THE ARCHIVE TODAY

Computers have now made it possible for Frith's many thousands of images to be accessed almost instantly. Frith's images are increasingly used as visual resources, by social historians, by researchers into genealogy and ancestry, by architects and town planners, and by teachers involved in local history projects.

In addition, the archive offers every one of us an opportunity to examine the places where we and our families have lived and worked down the years. Highly successful in Frith's own era, the archive is now, a century and more on, entering a new phase of popularity. Historians consider the Francis Frith Collection to be of prime national importance. It is the only archive of its kind remaining in private ownership. Francis Frith's archive is now housed in an historic timber barn in the beautiful village of Teffont in Wiltshire. Its founder would not recognize the archive office as it is today. In place of the many thousands of dusty boxes containing glass plate negatives and an all-pervading odour of photographic chemicals, there are now ranks of computer screens. He would be amazed to watch his images travelling round the world at unimaginable speeds through internet lines.

The archive's future is both bright and exciting. Francis Frith, with his unshakeable belief in making photographs available to the greatest number of people, would undoubtedly approve of what is being done today with his lifetime's work. His photographs depicting our shared past are now bringing pleasure and enlightenment to millions around the world a century and more after his death.

SCILLY ISLANDS

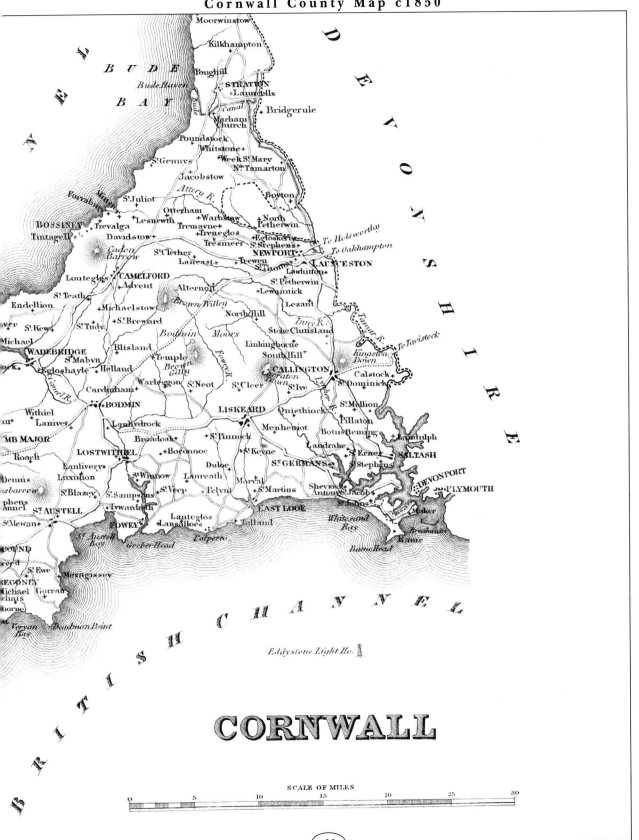

CORNWALL

SCALE OF MILES

0   5   10   15   20   25   30

THE CORNISH COAST - *An Introduction*

A CONDENSED HISTORY of this wild and beautiful coast might run thus: tin, pilchards, piracy, pilchards, tin, smuggling, more pilchards, more tin, and tourism. Throw in storms and shipwrecks, add a dash of war, famine and grinding poverty, season with all the human vices and an equal number of virtues, and you have a portrait of a land and people whose hopes, fears, achievements and failures are all inextricably linked with the sea.

The earliest known settlers of the Cornish coast were Bronze Age men and women in about 1500 BC. They and their Iron Age successors saw in headlands such as Pendinas at St Ives and Tintagel the security of easily defended high ground; they built forts there, an action that was to be echoed down the

centuries with the construction of forts like Pendennis and St Catherine's. Both Pendinas and Pendennis (and, for that matter, Pendeen) translate from the Cornish as 'fortified headland'. The Cornish language originated with the Celts, and is closely related to both Breton and Welsh. It died out as a mother tongue with Dolly Pentreath in 1777, but still lives on in thousands of names. There is an old rhyme which goes 'By Tre, Pol and Pen, Ye shall know Cornishmen', and these are the most common prefixes in Cornish names: 'Tre' meaning homestead or town, 'Pol' meaning pool, and 'Pen' headland or hill. The addition of another Cornish word completes the name: Polperro is 'Peter's Pool' and Treventon 'Town of the Spring'. Other common prefixes are

Porth (bay), Lan (enclosure, church) and Ros (heath).

Having their own language gave the Cornish a sense of cultural identity; this, combined with poor communication by land, the unforgiving nature of the coast and (arguably) a certain amount of sheer bloody-mindedness, led to successive rulers finding the unruly inhabitants of Britain's far south-west something of a headache. The Romans never succeeded in quelling the Celts, English monarchs such as Henry I had to reign with a firm hand, Edward IV had problems with the pirates of Fowey, and as late as the 18th century smugglers were operating as a law unto themselves.

The Cornish independence of spirit might have been overlooked or even indulged by the powers of the day were it not for Cornwall's strategic importance guarding the Western Approaches and its mineral wealth in the shape of tin and later copper. There is evidence that the Phoenicians were making the long journey from the Mediterranean to trade for tin as early as 500 BC. The trading post where they landed was called Ictis, and its exact location is the source of some argument; St Michael's Mount would seem to have a good claim to the name, but then so has Mountbatten in Plymouth. It has also been suggested that St Mawes did business with the Phoenicians.

Tin was far from being the only commodity moving around the coast, however; in fact, it was probably dwarfed by the huge volume of hides, grain, timber, coal, boots, cooking pots and all manner of chattels that were constantly in movement on what was the county's major highway. Inland, hills and moorland were a very real barrier to travel, and the quickest way to move objects and people from, say, Penzance to Padstow was by sea, despite the dangers of a passage around Lands End. Ports such as Truro, Lostwithiel and Wadebridge had the advantage of lying at the head of navigable estuaries up which cargoes could be shipped some distance inland.

The sea provided not only a reasonably reliable (if risky) means of travel, but also a vital source of food. Men (for fishing was considered man's work, women being fit only for the gutting of the catch) have been putting to sea to harvest the rich waters off the Cornish coast ever since it was settled. Almost every village on the coast has a long history of fishing. Some, such as Polperro, Portloe and Boscastle, are tiny natural harbours sheltered by cliffs, but others had no natural shelter. Newquay's old Cornish name is Tewynplustri, which translates as 'boat cove in the sandhills'. Fishermen here had to launch their gigs through the surf directly from the beach before the harbour was built in the 15th century. Life was 'nasty, brutish and short' as Thomas Hobbes wrote

in 'Leviathan' in the 17th century. A sharp summer storm could decimate a fleet caught out at sea, and the physical demands of working a fishing gig or lugger and hauling in the catch were enormous.

The rewards, too, could be enormous. Vast shoals of pilchards swarmed round the coast, and would be fished by up to fifty boats operating in unison to ring the shoal with their seine nets, occasionally pulling in a million fish in a day. Sometimes the shoals did not appear, and the locals would be reduced to scraping a living - literally - from the shore in the form of limpets and mussels, but when the fishing was good everybody ate well and vast quantities of pilchards were salted for export and to feed the Royal Navy. So important was the pilchard fishery considered that in the 18th century the Admiralty released an edict that no pilchard men were to be pressed into naval service.

The skills of Cornish seafarers enabled them to travel far and wide. They crewed and skippered trading schooners, Fowey fishermen roved as far as the Grand Banks off Newfoundland, and at least one Cornishman is known to have accompanied Drake on his circumnavigation of the globe. With the adaptability common to all people who live and work in a hostile and fickle environment, the Cornish were able to employ their skills and knowledge to make the best of any opportunity

that came along. They were not averse to the odd bit of piracy, and should a ship be blown onto the rocks it seemed common sense that the remains of the wreck and its cargo should be shared out among the community. Whether Cornish wreckers ever actually lured ships onto the rocks with lanterns masquerading as navigation lights is doubtful, but the concept of 'Wreckers Rights' was taken for granted; as late as the 1980s there was a case of a shipwreck that was stripped of everything of use.

Cornwall's most romanticised industry was smuggling. In reality it was a grim and dangerous affair, for amplifying the usual hazards of any venture at sea was the fact that it usually had to be undertaken in darkness - and in addition there was the risk of a brush with the law. There was little love lost between the Revenue Men and the smugglers; clashes between them could be vicious and the penalties were severe, although sometimes mitigated by the connivance of the clergy, landowners and even magistrates. Smuggling arose as a response to what were seen as punitive duties on a range of commodities, and the trade involved export as well as import - in Elizabethan times both tin and wool were smuggled across the channel. The heyday of smuggling was in the 18th and early 19th centuries when, according to one estimate, upwards of 40,000 people were involved; but by 1830 a determined campaign

by the authorities in the shape of a coastal blockade had almost eradicated the trade, and smugglers had returned to more lawful pursuits.

Mines were producing huge quantities of tin and copper, and powerful mineowners such as Thomas Treffry were buying whole harbours in order to ship ores to the smelters of South Wales. Larger harbours like Newquay (today home to thirty or forty small fishing boats) might have eight 100-ton schooners in port at any one time, and apparently inhospitable sites such as Trevaunance Cove had their own little harbours.

The pilchard men were still busy, hauling in vast catches, but in the 1870s the pilchard stocks crashed and never recovered to their former levels. Times were hard, but the timely arrival of the railways and the development of a prosperous middle class who liked to take their holidays by the sea presented an opportunity that the ever-adaptable Cornish grasped with both hands. With the dawn of the 20th century tourism boomed - hotels, tea-rooms, souvenir shops and holiday homes mushroomed all along the coast, often to the detriment of its natural beauty.

As tourism grew, so the mines declined, and today all that remains of this once great industry are the gaunt ruins of the engine houses that stand watch over the clifftops and moorland.

The fish cellars that once stored catch and nets have largely disappeared, but the fleet fishes on in harbours like Newlyn and Polperro and tiny coves such as Cadgwith, struggling against dwindling stocks and competition from foreign boats. Alongside the sturdy trawlers, crabbers and longliners today are moored private yachts and pleasure craft, and while the paraphernalia of tourism is evident everywhere, the tiny cottages that cling to the steep hillsides remain outwardly unchanged. Away from human habitation ravens wheel over the cliffs and gannets dive for fish, grey seals give birth to their pups in isolated coves, and if you are lucky you may catch sight of a school of dolphins or even pilot whales.

The rhythms of life continue in tandem with those of the seasons and the moods of the sea; fisherman, tourist and hotel owner alike still have their activities governed by storm and calm, sun and rain, winter and summer. The bad season for the tourist trade is an echo of the crash of the pilchard stocks or falling tin prices. Sail may have given way to diesel and tin to postcards and souvenir tee-shirts, but the unpredictable Atlantic weather system still writes the script.

The North Coast

MORWENSTOW
The Bush Inn c1955 M100003
The vast parish of Morwenstow's most famous Rector was
Robert Stephen Hawker, incumbent from 1834-75. He
was also a poet and songwriter and wrote 'The Song of the
Western Men', Cornwall's national song. The Bush Inn, half
a mile from the church, still stands, but now has a slate roof
after the thatch was destroyed in a fire in 1968.

BUDE, THE HARBOUR 1890 23782X

The Bude Canal, in which these schooners are moored, was built in 1823 to carry sand inland to improve farmland, but it ended up carrying all manner of cargoes including coal from South Wales. It had an impressive system of inclined planes to deal with the hills inland, but fell into disuse; today only the short seaward end is in use.

BUDE, EFFORD COTTAGE 1890 23784

Efford Cottage was built in 1823 by Sir Thomas Acland as a summer home. It stands below Efford Down, on top of which is the Storm Tower, also built by Acland. Octagonal in shape, its eight sides once matched the cardinal and sub-cardinal points of the compass, but polar drift has meant that the sides no longer align.

BUDE, THE LIFEBOAT 1890 23798

The schooner anchored here, awaiting high tide to allow it to enter the canal, is the 'President Garfield'. The lifeboat is the third one to be stationed at Bude, the 'Elizabeth Moore Garden 2'. Launching at low tide was achieved by towing the boat over the sand with a team of horses; the launch took place stern first to protect the rudder in the surf.

BUDE
Hartland Terrace 1890

Built on the opposite side of the beach to the harbour in the mid 19th century, Hartland Terrace still has some of its original buildings despite the encroachment of hotels.

BUDE
The Bathing Beach 1920

Bathing has not always been the family pastime it is today. 'Tommy's Pit', built at the end of the breakwater, was strictly men only, while women used Crooklets beach, then named Maer Beach. Mixed bathing did not come about until after World War One.

BUDE, HARTLAND TERRACE 1890 23808

BUDE, THE BATHING BEACH 1920 69503

BUDE, BARREL ROCK 1893 31915
Barrel Rock (centre right, with the marker post) marks the end of Bude's breakwater. The first one was destroyed in a storm in 1838 and was replaced by one designed by James Walker. The top is only four feet above high water at spring tides, but its shallow incline has enabled it to survive the worst the Atlantic can throw at it.

CRACKINGTON HAVEN, LOOKING SOUTH 1920 69530
Crackington Haven, six miles south of Bude, sits in a deep valley in the parish of St Gennys. An ancient settlement whose manor, a mile inland, is mentioned in the Domesday Book, it looks completely different today. The hillside on the left is now heavily built up.

CRACKINGTON HAVEN, THE VILLAGE 1931 84324
Specimens of 'Little Trees', a species of deep water coral so named because of its shape, are sometimes washed up on the beach at Crackington. Local lore says that they are a good luck charm, and that having a piece in your house will prevent it burning down.

BOSCASTLE, THE HARBOUR 1894 33612

The deep inlet of Boscastle Harbour is one of the few safe anchorages on this exposed coast. Its narrowness and the fact that it is surrounded by high cliffs make it very difficult to spot from the sea, and a winding inlet has to be negotiated before the harbour can be reached.

BOSCASTLE, THE WELLINGTON HOTEL 1906 56171

The Wellington Hotel, still in business today, was one of the last posting houses in the country, with stage coaches running into the 1920s. In 1849 the coach from Saltash took nine hours; it would cost 4s 6d if you rode inside, 3s 4d if you were willing to brave the weather outside. The road journey from Saltash today takes about an hour and a half.

BOSCASTLE, THE VILLAGE 1906 56168
Boscastle's steep, narrow roads with their tricky hairpins have reduced the impact of development; Old Hill looks
much the same today as it did in 1906. Local opinion is that the village is every bit as striking as the more famous
Clovelly in nearby North Devon.

BOSCASTLE, PIXIE COTTAGE c1960 B149106
Boscastle's slate-built cottages cling to the side of the beautiful valley of the River Valency, an important route inland down which came the slate and grain that were shipped from the harbour.

TINTAGEL 1894 33597
Despite the Arthurian legends attached to Tintagel, it seems doubtful that Camelot was actually here. There is no denying the power of the remains of the medieval castle on the 270-foot-high island, however - or their pulling power for visitors.

TINTAGEL, THE VILLAGE 1906 56178

Today, as in 1906, Tintagel makes a good living from the tourist, although now the currency in question is as likely to be the dollar or the yen as pounds sterling. Visitors can stay at the King Arthur's Castle Hotel where once, no doubt, Arthur entertained Guinevere, or queue for fish and chips in the same establishment once patronised by the Knights of the Round Table.

TINTAGEL, THE OLD POST OFFICE 1895 36990

One of Tintagel's most famous buildings, the Old Post Office dates from the 14th century and was used as a post office in the 19th century. It fell into disrepair in the early part of the 20th century, but it has now been completely restored by the National Trust.

PORT ISAAC, GENERAL VIEW 1895 37023

The ship on the beach is typical of the two-masted coastal schooners that plied their trade in the days before motor vehicles came to be used for the moving of commodities. They were loaded and unloaded either on foot or by horse and cart - a horse can be seen waiting at the port side of the vessel.

PORT ISAAC, THE HARBOUR 1903 49843

The harbour here is sheltered by Lobber Point (left) from the prevailing westerlies; although it is wider and easier to navigate than Boscastle, say, it still presented problems for schooners such as that in picture No 37023. In any sort of swell (the usual conditions on this coast), setting sail was a tricky business.

PORT ISAAC, THE HARBOUR 1920 69688
Fishing was Port Isaac's living for many centuries, and the staple was, as for so many other Cornish ports, pilchards.
These small luggers worked co-operatively with seine nets to ring the huge shoals, aided by 'Huers' on the cliffs who
directed the fleet with horns and flags.

PORT ISAAC, FORE STREET 1906 56182
Another important source of income for the locals was smuggling. In this they were aided by Port Isaac's maze of
narrow streets, or 'drangs', in which they could run the excise men ragged, communicating by a series of coded
knocks on the walls of adjoining houses.

PORT ISAAC, THE VILLAGE 1938 88790
Port Isaac made front page news in 1999 when local farmer Robert Sloman's Landrover went out of control on the steep hill behind the village. The occupants jumped to safety, but the Landrover buried itself in the roof of a house below; from there it had to be removed piecemeal, as the site was too inaccessible to use a crane.

POLZEATH, THE SANDS 1895 37020

POLZEATH
The Sands 1895
Hayle Bay, with its lines of evenly-breaking surf and golden sand, is now a mecca for surfers and tourists, and New Polzeath has grown along the low cliffs on the opposite side of the beach. The prominent headland is Pentire Point, home to some of the finest rock-climbs in the country.

POLZEATH
The Terrace 1911
This fine Edwardian terrace, with its breathtaking views, would not long have been completed when this photograph was taken. It stands at the top of the low cliffs visible in photograph No 86689.

POLZEATH, THE TERRACE 1911 63713

POLZEATH, THE BEACH 1935 86689

Unusual things have been found on the beach at Polzeath: in 1796 a 65-foot whale was washed up and the carcase used for manure, while in January 1866 280 casks of rum from the wreck of the 'Juliet' landed here. 'General drunkenness' resulted, apparently.

ROCK, THE FERRY c1960 R45017
The estuary of the Camel is one of Cornwall's greatest natural features, fringed with golden sands and surrounded by rolling farmland. The Camel rises north of Camelford on the edge of Bodmin Moor, and is one of Cornwall's best salmon rivers - a 34lb specimen was caught in the twenties.

ROCK, THE VILLAGE 1933 85987
Rock lies opposite Padstow (background) on the shore of the Camel estuary. Today it is a popular spot for the sailing fraternity, and the sailing club now occupies the area of corrugated shacks on the left. The black Rolls Royce is common in Frith's pictures from this time on - perhaps it belonged to the photographer.

PADSTOW, GENERAL VIEW 1894 33573
The harbour at Padstow originally belonged to Bodmin Priory and has had many celebrated visitors, none more so, perhaps, than Sir Walter Raleigh, who used it frequently when he was Lord Warden of the Stannaries in the 16th century.

PADSTOW
Church Chapel Stile 1901
Although it is sheltered and here looks relatively tranquil, the estuary has claimed many ships. The famous Doom Bar (so famous it even has a beer named after it!) extends from the west shore for nearly half a mile; in a big swell and falling tide it becomes a vicious mass of white water.

PADSTOW
The Railway Bridge 1906
The branch line from Wadebridge runs along the southern shore of the estuary; the first train ran on 23 March 1899. The last train was on 28 January 1967, and the line is now the Camel Trail, a superb cycleway. The bridge in the picture is just south of Padstow.

PADSTOW, CHURCH CHAPEL STILE 1901 47720

PADSTOW, THE RAILWAY BRIDGE 1906 56273

HARLYN BAY c1955 T78001

HARLYN BAY c1955
The horseshoe-shaped Harlyn Bay is one of the
county's best beaches, much favoured by picnickers
and surfers. Beyond the headland in the background
is Trevose Head, topped by its lighthouse which is
visible from many miles out to sea.

HARLYN BAY
Prehistoric Settlement 1901 47727
These Edwardian ladies are looking at the Iron Age
cemetery that was discovered here in 1900. A major
find, with 130 graves, the dig was supervised by a Mr
Reddie Mallet and one of the diggers was the Rev
Sabine Baring-Gould, writer of 'Onward
Christian Soldiers'.

HARLYN BAY, PREHISTORIC SETTLEMENT 1901 47727

HARLYN BAY, THE VILLAGE 1923 74878
Prior to tourism and archaeology, Harlyn was a fishing village. The fleet fished mainly for pilchards using seine nets but, like fishermen the world over, would catch anything they could sell or eat - in May 1888 a Mr Saunders harpooned a young Sperm Whale.

ST COLUMB, FAIR STREET 1906 56242
St Columb's most famous son was James Polkinghorne, who divided his time between being landlord of the Red Lion and participating in Cornish wrestling. This was once a major sport: Polkinghorne, as Cornish Champion, fought in front of a crowd of 17,000 when he faced Devon Champion Abraham Cann in 1826.

BEDRUTHAN STEPS, THE OLD STEPS 1935 86720

These huge foreshore stacks, one of Cornwall's most famous sights, were formed by the erosion of softer rocks around them. More romantic is the legend that states that these rocks were stepping-stones used by the giant Bedruthan.

MAWGAN PORTH, GENERAL VIEW 1935 87135

The stream here flows through the Vale of Mawgan from St Columb. A couple of miles inland is the Village of St Mawgan, from which the giant airbase takes its name. A memorial in the churchyard commemorates the ten crew of a ship that froze to death in a lifeboat in 1846.

WATERGATE BAY, THE BEACH c1955 W38012
In the background is the Watergate Bay Hotel, at this time in use as RAF married quarters, having been requisitioned at the outbreak of World War Two. It spent some time empty when the RAF left before being converted to holiday flats and eventually re-opening as a hotel in 1971.

PORTH, THE VILLAGE AND THE SANDS 1887 20284
This schooner may well have been unloading limestone, which was shipped from South Wales to be fired in the lime-kiln that still stands at the side of the beach. The lime was then taken inland to regulate the acidity of the soil.

PORTH, THE VILLAGE 1935 86713
This photograph was taken in the year that Giles Gilbert Scott designed the much-loved red telephone box, which was soon to become a familiar sight all over the country. Oddly enough, it appears that the old box in this picture was not replaced by a red one.

PORTH, THE SANDS C1950 P78037

Changing times - instead of a schooner on the beach, there is a fine parade of classic cars - but look carefully and the old telephone box is still there. Behind the wall to the left of the telephone box was once Stephen's yard, used for storing cargoes.

NEWQUAY, THE SANDS 1894 33516

The prominent hotel on the headland is the Atlantic, and just to its right is the Huer's Hut, where the huers watched for the pilchard shoals. The name comes from the Cornish 'heva', meaning 'found', which the huer would shout on sighting a shoal.

NEWQUAY
THE BEACON 1894 33525
The Beacon, just south of the Atlantic Hotel (in the background) was once a Coastguard lookout. Its place is now occupied by the town war memorial, which incorporates the lookout in its structure.

NEWQUAY, NARROWCLIFF 1899 43169
Here we see Newquay at the beginning of the building boom which was to turn Narrowcliff into the largest concentration of hotel rooms in the county. The horse and cart appear to be delivering building stone.

NEWQUAY, THE SANDS 1901 47733
We are looking north-west across Towan Beach towards the harbour, one of the more sheltered on this exposed coast, built in the lee of Towan Head which protects it from the brunt of the ferocious Atlantic westerlies.

PENTIRE, THE SANDS FROM FERNPIT TEA GARDENS C1955 P359005

PENTIRE
The Sands from Fernpit Tea Gardens c1955
Fern Pit, at the mouth of the Gannel, was owned
by generations of Northeys, who also ran the ferry
to Crantock, which is in the background on the
other side of Crantock Beach. Crantock was once a
favoured haunt of smugglers.

PERRANPORTH
The Hotel 1890
Perranporth takes its name from St Piran, patron
saint of Cornish miners, and was originally a mining
community. It received its first taste of tourism as
early as the 1800s, when Truronians used to come
here to paddle.

PERRANPORTH, THE HOTEL 1890 23967

PERRANPORTH, FROM THE SANDHILLS 1893 31821

The sandhills to the north of Perranporth are constantly shifting; they are held in check by marram grass, reputed to have been introduced by Sir Walter Raleigh. The dunes hide St Piran's Oratory, Cornwall's famous 'lost church', built in the 7th century and covered by the sands.

PERRANPORTH, THE ROCKS 1912 64836

The cliffs to the south of Perranporth are riddled with the adits of old mine workings, which followed the rich veins of tin and copper that ran from the granite intrusion of Cligga Head into the surrounding Killas slate.

ST AGNES, THE CLIFF SHELTER C1955 S390032

First built in 1632 and rebuilt another four times, the harbour at St Agnes was small and had a tricky entrance, but thrived on business from the mines before falling into disrepair and finally succumbing to the Atlantic between 1914 and 1920.

PORTHTOWAN, GENERAL VIEW 1925 78613

Another ex-mining settlement, Porthtowan became a popular destination for day-trippers from Redruth around the turn of the century. It boasted four tea-rooms just inland from the beach - they are visible on the right fork of the road in this picture.

PORTREATH, A ROUGH SEA c1965 P95018E
Portreath's first pier was built in 1760 by Francis Basset, a member of one of Cornwall's most prominent mining families. Ore was taken to the smelters of South Wales, and the same ships returned with coal to power the mines.

PORTREATH, GENERAL VIEW c1955 P95001

PORTREATH
General View c1955

Portreath was once a thriving little mining port at the terminus of Cornwall's first (horse-drawn) railway. Ships visited until the 1960s, but today the village is totally given over to the tourist trade.

GODREVY ISLAND
The Lighthouse 1890

The loss in 1854 of the 700 ton steamer the 'Nile' with all aboard caused an enormous outcry; as a result the octagonal lighthouse on Godrevy Island was built. It lies a quarter of a mile off Godrevy Point.

GODREVY ISLAND, THE LIGHTHOUSE 1890 24194

GODREVY LIGHTHOUSE 1890 24195
Virginia Woolf was a frequent visitor to Cornwall and her most famous novel, 'To the Lighthouse', was inspired by Godrevy. The lighthouse is no longer manned; it is now powered by solar panels, which occupy what used to be the keepers' garden.

GWITHIAN, THE PENDARVES ARMS C1960 G187041
Gwithian Towans, the three-mile stretch of sandhills in which the village stands, was from 1889-1920 the home of the National Explosives works, which produced much of the cordite used in artillery shells during World War One. It employed 1,800 people who worked in small enclosures sunk into the dunes and isolated from each other to prevent a disastrous chain reaction in the event of an explosion or fire.

Penwith

CARBIS BAY
The Hotel 1898 41614
Before the arrival of the hotel in 1894, Carbis Bay was known as
Carbis Valley. One of the few houses was Hawkes Point Cottage,
seen here (right) on the nearest headland. The four-and-a-half
mile St Erth to St Ives branch line (visible on the left) saw its first
train in 1877.

CARBIS BAY, DONKEY RIDES 1928 81192
Where have all the donkeys gone? Once a common sight on the beaches of the south-west, they have long since disappeared. The distant headland is Godrevy Point, with Godrevy Island just visible to its left.

ST IVES, GENERAL VIEW 1898 35831
For centuries a fishing port, St Ives is today better known for its artistic community. Artists such as Christopher Wood, Ben Nicholson, Barbara Hepworth, Peter Lanyon and Patrick Heron all lived and worked here, making use of the unique quality of Penwith's light.

ST IVES
THE CHAPEL OF ST NICHOLAS 1892
31161A
St Ives Island, on which the Chapel of St Nicholas stands, is actually a headland joined to the shore. Its Cornish name of Pendinas means 'fortified headland', and for centuries that was what it was - there are the remains of an Iron Age fort, and the island once held guns to ward off the threat from Napoleon's forces.

ST IVES, HICKS COURT 1892 29873
St Ives has many small courtyards like this, which would once have been a centre for domestic and social life. The enormous granite lintel and gatepost might once have held a sturdy door which could be shut against unwelcome visitors.

ST IVES, THE HARBOUR 1892 29870

St Ives Harbour, facing east and in the lee of the Island, is one of the more sheltered harbours on this rugged coastline. The harbour wall was built in 1770 by John Smeaton, who in 1759 built the fourth Eddystone Lighthouse which now stands on Plymouth Hoe. The old St Ives light (far left) was also designed by Smeaton.

ST IVES, THE ISLAND 1890 24180

The Island stands at the western end of Porthmeor Beach, visible behind the ruined mine building. Today Porthmeor Beach is home to the Tate Gallery St Ives, built on the site of the old gasholder which can just be seen to the right of the ruin.

ZENNOR
the Village 1928
Zennor is home to one of Cornwall's more picturesque legends - that of the mermaid of Zennor. On hearing her sing in the church, one Matthew Trewhella fell in love with her, followed her to the sea and was never heard of again.

◆

CAPE CORNWALL 1890
Cornwall's only cape lies almost as far west as Land's End; lacking any tourist apparatus, it is a beautiful and quiet headland. The chimney at the summit is that of the Cape Cornwall mine, whose workings ran far out under the sea to the north-west.

ZENNOR, THE VILLAGE 1928 81229

CAPE CORNWALL 1890 27744

LANDS END AND THE LONGSHIPS LIGHTHOUSE c1955 L13032

3147 miles from New York, England's most westerly point was named Belerion, or Seat of Storms, by the Romans. Painted by (among others) Turner, written about by (among others) Ruskin, and with the Isles of Scilly visible on the horizon on a clear day, it is a dramatic place despite the hordes of tourists.

LANDS END AND THE ARMED KNIGHT ROCKS 1890 23073

The Longships Reef, two miles offshore, was a ships' graveyard until 1795, when the first lighthouse was built. It was replaced by the 112-foot present tower in 1873.

ST LEVAN, THE CHURCH 1908 61266

The 15th-century church is named after St Levan, said to have landed nearby in the 5th or 6th centuries. It lies not far from the famous Minack Theatre, cut from the cliffs in the thirties by Rowena Cade. The first production, in 1932, was 'The Tempest' - the perfect play to see in such a dramatic setting.

TREEN, THE VILLAGE c1955 T207009

Remove the old car, and the perfect little village of Treen would look exactly the same today. Down the hill to the left lie the delights of the Logan Rock Inn, while turning right after the telephone box leads to a beautiful campsite high above Porthcurno beach.

LOGAN ROCK AND THE SCILLY BOAT 1928 81244

LOGAN ROCK
and the Scilly Boat 1928
The 66 ton Logan Rock was forcibly dislodged
in 1824 by a Lt Goldsmith and the crew of the
Revenue Cutter 'Nimble'. Such was the outcry that
Goldsmith had to replace the rock at his own (not
inconsiderable) expense. The total bill came to
£130 8s 6d, some of which went to '60 men of
St Just who did nothing but drink beer
to the value of 13s 6d'.

◆

LAMORNA COVE
The Village 1927
One of Lamorna's most famous residents was the
painter Samuel John Birch, who moved there in
1892 and stayed for the rest of his life. Granite from
Lamorna was used in the building of the Thames
Embankment, the London County Council
Offices and Dover Pier.

LAMORNA COVE, THE VILLAGE 1927 79958

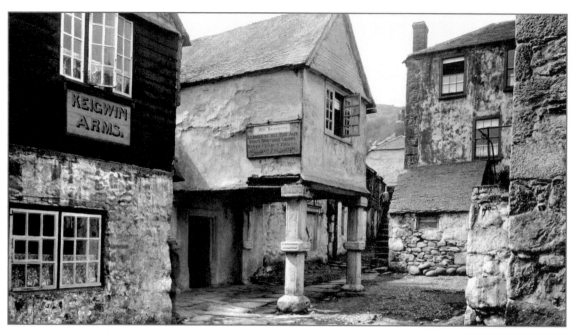

MOUSEHOLE, THE KEIGWIN ARMS 1893 31805

The Keigwin Arms takes its name from Jenkin Keigwin, a local squire killed by the Spaniards in 1595 when they sacked the town in revenge for the destruction of the Armada. Nearby is a memorial to Dolly Pentreath, the last speaker of Cornish as a mother tongue, who died in 1777 aged 102.

MOUSEHOLE, THE HARBOUR AND THE VILLAGE 1927 79945

Dylan Thomas tarried awhile in Mousehole and married his sweetheart Caitlin at Penzance Register Office in 1937. He described Mousehole as 'the loveliest village in England'. Who can argue with that?

MOUSEHOLE, THE HARBOUR 1927 79949
Mousehole (pronounced 'Mouzel') is an ancient village, the south pier having been first built in around 400 AD. For centuries it thrived as a fishing port, but it lost out with the rise of nearby Newlyn in the 19th century.

NEWLYN
THE FISH MARKET 1906 56524
Newlyn was the first Cornish town to attract the attention of artists. The Newlyn School numbered among its luminaries Henry Scott Tuke, Edwin Harris and William Wainwright, but the leading light was undoubtedly Stanhope Forbes, whose masterpiece 'Fish Sale on Newlyn Beach' can now be seen in Plymouth City Art Gallery.

NEWLYN, FISHERMEN'S COTTAGES 1903 50867

In 1896 Newlyn fishermen, who never put to sea on Saturdays or Sundays, rioted in protest at 200 Lowestoft boats who worked at weekends. 2,000 men barricaded the harbour, preventing the East Coast men from putting to sea, and threw fish over the side. The police could not cope, and 300 soldiers of the Royal Berkshire regiment had to be drafted in to restore order.

PENZANCE, THE ESPLANADE c1883 16022

Despite the relative shelter offered by Mounts Bay, winter storms can sometimes be ferocious. A particularly bad one on 7 October 1880 destroyed the promenade and also killed seven men on the Mousehole boat 'Jane'.

Penzance, A Fishwife 1890 27699
The wicker basket is called a cowal. Older fishwives would walk for miles carrying their cowals until the contents were all sold. Younger fishwives did not sell fish, but helped with the cleaning and salting of the catch.

PENZANCE, FISHING BOATS 1890 22978A

Penzance was 'a place of good business, well built and populous, having a good trade and a great many ships belonging to it', according to Daniel Defoe, when he visited in the 17th century. Today the ships are rather less numerous - the Isles of Scilly boat 'Scillonian' is the only vessel of any size to operate from the harbour.

PENZANCE, GULVAL CHURCH 1893 31791

Penzance harbour is in the middle distance. The farthest headland is Penlee Point, home of the lifeboat 'Solomon Browne', which was lost with all hands in December 1981 during a gallant attempt to rescue the crew of the coaster 'Union Star' in a winter storm.

PENZANCE, ON THE ROCKS 1906 56513

The church in the distance is that of St Mary, built in 1833. In the centre is the Mounts Bay Hotel (right) and the Queen's Hotel (left, with turret). On the far left is the as yet empty site of the Pavilion, which was to be built in 1911.

MARAZION, FORE STREET 1920 69755

The origins of Marazion's name are the subject of some argument. One theory is that it comes from the Cornish for 'Market Jew', the Jews in question having arrived with the Romans or been brought by King John to work local mines. The name 'Market Jew' lives on in the name of nearby Penzance's main street.

MARAZION, ST MICHAEL'S MOUNT c1960 M26011
St Michael's Mount has been the home of the St Aubyn family since the 17th century, but it has been settled for many centuries and has a claim to be the legendary Ictis which traded tin with the Phoenicians; this history is also claimed by other sites on the south coast, notably Plymouth's Mountbatten.

PERRANUTHNOE
The Flower Fields c1955

At high tide the causeway to the mount is covered and access is by boat. The presence of the mount contributed to the growth of nearby Marazion, which flourished in its shadow and catered for the many pilgrims who came to the Benedictine priory which was built on the summit in 1135.

PRAA SANDS 1927

A mile to the west of Praa Sands is Prussia Cove, a narrow inlet which takes its name from John Carter, an 18th-century smuggler whose nickname was the King of Prussia. He ran the cove as his own fiefdom, and even mounted a battery of guns on the cliffs.

PERRANUTHNOE, THE FLOWER FIELDS c1955 P240003

PRAA SANDS 1927 79967

The Lizard & Falmouth

PORTHLEVEN
The Harbour 1924 76623
Porthleven's large harbour was built in 1811 to load copper and
tin; it is an important haven on the exposed east shore of Mount's
Bay. A good example of the ferocity of winter storms was in 1990,
when waves were breaking over the 70-foot tower of the Bickford
Smith Institute in the background.

◆

GUNWALLOE, THE CHURCH 1903 49936
The 15th-century church of St Winwaloe stands only yards from the shore of Church Cove; it contains timbers from the Portuguese galleon 'St Anthony', which was blown ashore in the cove in 1526.

MULLION, THE COVE AND THE HOTEL 1899 43797
The dramatic greenstone pinnacle of Gull Rock, or Scovarn, dominates the entrance to the cove, which is now owned by the National Trust. Mullion (named after St Melanus) was once a thriving fishing community, making a living from the ubiquitous pilchards in the autumn and lobster and crab in spring.

MULLION, THE PIER HEAD AND GULL ROCK 1899 43802
A fisherman's life was hard, even when the weather was kind: in 1872 William Munday, coxswain of the Mullion lifeboat, and his crew of three were lost on a fine spring day when their boat foundered in sight of Porthleven harbour. The loss 'cast a deep gloom over the whole of the community in which the unfortunate deceased resided'.

MULLION, THE GOLF LINKS 1911 64023
Polurrian Cove lies just north of Mullion Cove itself, and is the town's main beach. On the left is Polbream Point, round which a fine walk leads over Angrouse Cliff to Poldhu Cove.

MULLION, THE VILLAGE 1904 52261

The famous evangelist the Rev C H Spurgeon, who visited Mullion in 1872, was obviously impressed by the locals: 'If I were asked to select the Cornish parish which contains the greatest number of intelligent people, I should at once turn to Mullion'.

KYNANCE COVE 1890 24269

Kynans is Cornish for gorge, an appropriate name for this little cove, which even today is only approachable by a narrow, unmade track. On the far left is Asparagus Island, so named because asparagus used to grow there, and to its right is the prominent pinnacle of the Steeple.

THE LIZARD, THE PATH TO KYNANCE COVE 1927 80020
The path between Lizard and Kynance is part of the South West Coast Path, which for long stretches owes its existence to the feet of the ever watchful Customs men: in the 18th and 19th centuries, they patrolled the cliffs on the lookout for smugglers.

THE LIZARD, HOUSEL ROAD 1904 52239
It is thought that Lizard takes its name from 'Lazar', an old word for lepers, who by necessity had to live in isolated communities away from the rest of the population, a requirement amply met by this remote spot.

THE LIZARD, THE SERPENTINE INDUSTRY c1950 L62019
Serpentine - one of the many rocks that make up the complex geology of the Lizard Peninsula - is soft, attractive and easily worked into ornaments and even furniture. The industry received a boost in 1846 when Queen Victoria bought a serpentine table and set a fashion trend.

THE LIZARD, THE LIFEBOAT SLIP 1927 80006
This old lifeboat station was in Polpeor Cove at the very southern extremity of the peninsula, exposed to the full force of the Atlantic and littered with reefs. In 1961 the station moved to Kilcobben Cove on the more sheltered eastern side of the Lizard.

THE LIZARD, THE GREEN 1927 80015
The closest the railway ever reached to Britain's most southerly spot was Helston, eleven miles away, so visitors had either to come by car or take one of the excursion buses which were run from 1903 by the Great Western Railway.

THE LIZARD, THE LION'S DEN AND BUMBLE 1895 36220

The pinnacle on the left is Bumble, just offshore from the rocky headland of the Lion's Den. The rocks of the Lizard have claimed innumerable victims, and the first, coal-powered lighthouse was built in 1619 by Sir John Killigrew. Today's light shines a beam of over five million candlepower which can be seen from 21 miles away.

CADGWITH, THE DEVIL'S FRYING PAN 1890 24265

Just south of Cadgwith, the Devil's Frying Pan was once a vast sea-cave before the roof collapsed, leaving this enormous blow-hole over 200 feet deep. Eventually, the remains of the roof will also collapse, resulting in the type of narrow inlet known in Cornish as a zawn.

CADGWITH, MAIN STREET 1899 44184

This is an idyllic scene, which belies the harshness of life in Cornish fishing villages in past times. Apart from the obvious hazards of storms and wrecks, failure of the fish stocks for even one season could lead to starvation that was only marginally eased by scraping limpets from the shore.

CADGWITH, THE VILLAGE 1911 63988

Fishermen have launched from Cadgwith's shingle cove for centuries. The boats on view here are typical of the rowing gigs used before the advent of diesel engines - sturdy and seaworthy, and often with their middle thwarts missing to leave space for the enormous seine nets that were used to encircle shoals.

THE LIZARD, CARLEON COVE 1911 64001

Lying to seaward of Poltesco, the rocky little beach of Carleon Cove had its own pilchard fleet until the 19th century, when it became the home of the Lizard Serpentine Company. Power for the production of ornaments was provided by the waterwheel in the foreground. The headland in the distance is Black Head.

COVERACK, THE HARBOUR 1938 88564

Coverack's quay was built in 1723 by John Ellis from Penryn granite and serpentine. The name Coverack variously translates as 'wreck cove' or 'hideaway' - appropriate in view of the occupations of residents in past centuries.

COVERACK, THE HARBOUR c1960 C170052
Smuggling was a major industry in the 18th century, with vast quantities of contraband passing through little ports such as Coverack. In 1736 the Coverack Customs boat caught a smuggler carrying 150 ankers of spirits. An anker was eight and a half gallons, so the haul represented around 5,500 bottles - and that was not considered a large cargo!

CADGWITH, THE VILLAGE c1900 C2502
Even innocent-looking cottages like this were often involved in the smuggling trade. The walls were at least two feet thick and, in some buildings, even thicker - with handy hidden rooms that could be used to conceal both contraband and smugglers.

MANACCAN, GILLAN FROM ST GORRANS c1955 M19005

Gillan Creek, just south of the mouth of the Helford River, is remote enough for smuggling to have been carried on here into the late 19th century, long after the crackdown in the aftermath of the Napoleonic Wars which sounded the death knell for 'free trading', as it was euphemistically known.

MANACCAN, GILLAN c1960 M19030

Beyond Dennis Head, on the opposite shore, is the mouth of the Helford River, which runs inland for five miles to Gweek. Its heavily wooded creeks were a favourite venue for smugglers, and include perhaps the most famous inlet of all - Frenchman's Creek, made famous by Daphne du Maurier.

ST ANTHONY, THE SHORE c1960 S736008

St Anthony-in-Meneage is a tiny hamlet at the mouth of Gillan Creek. It has a beautiful 12th-century church reputed to have been built by shipwrecked Normans in thanks for their lives being spared.

FALMOUTH, PENNANCE POINT 1895 37045

This photograph was taken from Gyllyngvase Beach. In the middle distance is Swanpool Point; hidden beyond it is Swanpool Beach, another favoured smuggling spot. The large headland is Pennance Point, and in the distance Rosemullion Head is just visible.

FALMOUTH, THE GREEN BANK HOTEL 1890 24209
The Green Bank Hotel, on the south bank of the Penryn River, was built in 1785 to cash in on the trade brought to the town by the mail packets. It was from here that Kenneth Graham wrote the letters to his son which eventually became 'The Wind in the Willows'.

FALMOUTH, THE BAY 1908 61041

Standing proudly at the top of Pendennis Point is Pendennis Castle, built by Henry VIII to guard the approaches to the estuary of the Fal, one of Cornwall's great waterways. During the Civil War, Pendennis held out against the massed Parliamentarian forces for five months before surrendering.

FALMOUTH, FLUSHING FROM GREEN BANK 1893 31843

Flushing's quays were built by Dutch engineers in the 17th century; with the arrival of the Royal Mail Packets, it became a flourishing port with elegant houses occupied by naval officers. Today's residents are more likely to skipper an expensive pleasure vessel.

The South Coast
St Mawes to Fowey

ST MAWES
General View 1895 37049
Despite its relative isolation from the main mining areas, St Mawes
is thought to have been an early tin trading post. It also had the
distinction, following an Act of Parliament in 1562, of sending two
MPs to Parliament - voted in by an electorate of only twenty!

ST MAWES, THE CASTLE 1938 88813

Like its twin castle of Pendennis on the opposite side of the river mouth, St Mawes was built on the orders of Henry VIII to guard the entrance to Carrick Roads. Unlike Pendennis, however, it did not hold out heroically during the Civil War, but fell without a shot being fired: as all its guns faced seaward, it could not defend itself from a land assault.

VERYAN, THE ROAD TO THE BEACH c1955 V3041

Veryan, probably named after a saint with the improbable name of Symphorian, is one of the county's most beautiful villages, noted for its five round houses, built that way so that the devil could not find a corner in which to hide. It is said that if the church clock strikes before the start of the sermon, there will be a death in the parish within the week.

PORTLOE, THE BEACH AND THE VILLAGE c1955 P245003
The village of Portloe (meaning 'bay with pool') is one of Cornwall's best-kept secrets - a tiny, rocky fishing cove with narrow streets and the fine 17th-century Lugger Inn. The cove faces east and is therefore relatively sheltered, but in 1959 an extra sea wall was built.

GORRAN HAVEN, THE HARBOUR 1890 27562
The characteristic square block of the fish cellars just above the two gigs in the picture betrays Gorran Haven's past as a fishing village. It was also known for boatbuilding - vessels built at Dick Pill's boatyard in the late 19th and early 20th centuries were highly regarded, and were used as far away as the east coast.

GORRAN HAVEN
The Church 1922

The Church of St Just has a 15th-century tower which was built to hold a light for shipping. This may have helped local boats, but the nearby Dodman Point claimed many ships. A granite cross on the Dodman was erected in 1896 by a local clergyman in the hope of encouraging the second coming.

◆

GORRAN CHURCHTOWN,
The Village 1890

Gorran Churchtown, a mile or so inland from Gorran Haven and nearly 300 feet above sea level, has a 15th-century church, the tower of which is an important mark for coastal shipping. Just round the corner from the terrace on the left used to be the stables for the horses of the mailcart from St Austell.

GORRAN HAVEN, THE CHURCH 1922 73313

GORRAN CHURCHTOWN, THE VILLAGE 1890 27566

MEVAGISSEY, THE HARBOUR FROM THE PIER 1890 27550
Originally known as Porthilly, Mevagissey was renamed after Saints Meva and Itha. Its first pier was built in the 15th century, but the town really grew in Napoleon's times, when it doubled in size owing to the fishing and smuggling boom.

MEVAGISSEY, FORE STREET 1890 27558
Mevagissey's steep, winding streets and alleys, cobbled with beach stone, formed a useful maze in which smugglers could escape the attentions of the revenue men. The building in the background with the white sheet is the premises of Alma Robins, Milliner and Draper.

MEVAGISSEY, THE HARBOUR 1904 52248

Mevagissey's huge fishing fleet comprised locally-built luggers, known for their speed and therefore very unpopular with the revenue men. Mevagissey pilchards were supplied dried to the Royal Navy and known as 'Mevagissey Ducks'.

PENTEWAN, THE VILLAGE 1904 52244

The long terrace of cottages is known locally as The Row; it once housed local workers, but it is now holiday homes. The Bible Christian Chapel (centre) with the schoolroom beneath it was built in 1889 and bombed in August 1942.

PENTEWAN, THE HARBOUR 1927 79874

Pentewan Harbour was built between 1819 and 1826 by Sir Christopher Hawkins. China clay from the St Austell pits was brought to the harbour by trains, which carried coal for the gasworks on the return journey. Unfortunately, clay runoff silted up the harbour and it closed after World War Two.

PORTHPEAN, THE BEACH C1955 P87005

Porthpean ('little bay') has always been the local beach for St Austell people. Its regatta was an annual attraction, and it still has a thriving sailing club. Behind the trees on the left is Porthpean House, home of the Petherick family.

PORTHPEAN, GENERAL VIEW 1890 27636

The cliffs below the road in the foreground were the scene in 1952 of two notorious murders. Miles Gifford killed his parents with a length of pipe after an argument over the use of their car, and then dumped their bodies over the cliff from a wheelbarrow. He was tried at Bodmin and hung.

CHARLESTOWN, THE HARBOUR 1904 53050

Built by Charles Rashleigh and designed by the ubiquitous John Smeaton, Charlestown was once one of Cornwall's busiest ports, shipping tin from the Polgooth Mine which in 1790 was the biggest in Cornwall. Between 1794 and 1874, 28 ships were built here, the largest being the 'Pride of the Channel' at 175 tons.

CARLYON BAY 1930 83204
On the skyline is the Carlyon Bay Hotel which, when completed in 1930, was one of the fashionable spots to stay, with guests that included Edward VIII and Mrs Simpson. The beach itself is now home to the Cornwall Coliseum.

PAR BAY, THE BEACH 1927 79886
Par Harbour was built in 1830 by mineowner Thomas Treffry, known as the 'King of mid-Cornwall'. Treffry used the harbour for shipping tin and copper, but china clay soon took over; since 1946 it has been run by English China Clays, and is now the busiest port per foot of quay in the UK.

PAR BAY, THE BEACH HUTS 1938 88578

In the background are two liquid china clay storage tanks. In the days before environmental concerns, both Par Beach and nearby Carlyon Bay were badly polluted by white, sticky clay runoff; as late as the seventies, it was clogging family washing machines after a day on the beach.

POLKERRIS, THE VILLAGE c1876 8449

Another fishing village, Polkerris had one of the largest fish cellars in Cornwall, so big that it was known as a fish palace. This is now the Rashleigh Arms, named after the family who still own the village and live at nearby Menabilly House, immortalised as Manderley by Daphne du Maurier in her book 'Rebecca'.

POLKERRIS, THE POST OFFICE c1955 P65019

POLKERRIS
The Post Office c1955
Polkerris's heyday was in the 19th century, when the
pilchard stocks still flourished. Today it is smaller
than in the past and many of the cottages are
holiday homes. The Post Office closed in June 1990
because of the decline in trade.

FOWEY
Ready Money Cove 1893
This picture is taken from near St Catherine's
Castle, built in 1538 by Thomas Treffry on orders
from Henry VIII. Just out of the picture on the right
is Point Neptune, an Italianate villa built by
William Rashleigh.

FOWEY, READY MONEY COVE 1893 32549

FOWEY, THE HARBOUR 1913 65962

Fowey seamen have been well travelled for centuries - as early as the 16th century they were working Newfoundland's grand banks for cod. Not all activities were legal, however - Edward IV had to pay off some European kings and princes after Fowey pirates stole ships and cargoes. The pirates were executed.

The South Coast
Fowey to Kingsand

BODINNICK
The Ferry Inn 1888 21236
Bodinnick lies opposite and slightly upstream of Fowey at the narrowest point of the estuary of the River Fowey.
The ferry from which the pub takes its name is one of Cornwall's more quaint river crossings - a wooden raft
powered by a boat tied alongside.

BODINNICK, FROM FOWEY 1888 21243

The River Fowey is one of Cornwall's longest rivers, rising 900 feet above sea level on Bodmin Moor and passing through the ancient Stannary Town of Lostwithiel on its way to the sea. The estuary provides a sheltered natural harbour, and in the past schooners such as the one here were a common sight.

POLRUAN, FROM FOWEY 1908 60925

Polruan was once a major shipbuilding port; in the 19th century it launched over 6,000 tons of shipping. The blockhouse on the shore to the right was the castle from where a chain was stretched across the river for protection in times of war. Not that it always worked - in 1457 a Breton fleet broke through and sacked Fowey.

POLRUAN
The Arrival of the Ferry c1955
Piloting, pilchards, piracy and privateering - anything nautical could provide a living for the seafarers of Polruan. Today there is still a flourishing boatyard, and the ferries ply their trade to Fowey opposite.

POLPERRO
General View 1888
Polperro is the archetypal Cornish fishing village - a higgledy-piggledy maze of narrow streets leading down to a perfect, tiny harbour. The east-facing harbour entrance is sheltered from westerlies, but in 1824 a mighty easterly storm demolished the breakwaters and wrecked the fleet, a disaster from which it took the village a long time to recover.

POLRUAN, THE ARRIVAL OF THE FERRY c1955 P69009

POLPERRO, GENERAL VIEW 1888 21265

POLPERRO, COUCH'S HOUSE 1924 76313

POLPERRO
Couch's House 1924
Polperro's narrow valley is particularly prone to
flash floods; in the drought summer of 1976 a
sudden downpour changed the stream into a raging
torrent which threw cars around like corks and
deposited several feet of mud in the streets. Flood
relief works alleviated the threat, but in 1994 the
village was again struck by flooding.

POLPERRO
A Promising Recruit 1907
The Royal Navy may well have recruited in Polperro,
but here, as with the rest of Cornwall, they took
only willing recruits. The pilchard fisheries were
considered so important that an Admiralty edict of
the 18th century stated that no pilchard men were
to be press-ganged.

POLPERRO, A PROMISING RECRUIT 1907 59268

TALLAND BAY 1924 76317

This was yet another popular spot with smugglers, who often ensured the silence of the local parson with the odd cask of brandy. Just visible on the open ground to the right of the church is one of the end markers of the measured nautical mile used once by ships undergoing sea trials; the other end marker is half a mile before Looe.

LOOE, FROM THE BRIDGE 1893 32374

During the 19th century, Looe was an important copper port; the proceeds from this trade paid for the fine Guildhall just visible on the left. Today, Looe is a fishing and tourist town. Buller's Quay in the foreground is now a car park, and the fish market is at the far end of the quay.

SEATON, THE BEACH 1920 69884
The cliff on the right now has a row of houses at the top. These were threatened by the instability of the cliffs, and in the 1980s a large sea wall was built, stretching from around the point out of the picture on the right. The valley of the River Seaton runs inland from the beach to Hessenford.

DOWNDERRY, THE VILLAGE 1894 34895
The house on the right, outside which the rather formidable-looking woman is standing, is reputed to be the oldest in Downderry. The subject of her conversation with the equally stern-looking woman with the donkey cart is probably not last night's party.

DOWNDERRY
CAVE DWELLERS 1901 47803
Frith may have been guilty of a little artistic licence in describing these women as 'cave dwellers' - there are indeed plenty of caves on the beach here, but all are sea-washed at high tide with even a small swell running. Perhaps these hard-looking women only spent the odd couple of days in the caves gathering flotsam and jetsam.

DOWNDERRY, THE COASTGUARD BUNGALOWS 1901 47799
These charming cottages still stand, altered but recognisable and now holiday homes. The village slipway, up and down which fishing boats are still hauled to protect them from winter storms, is down the road to the left.

CRAFTHOLE, WHITSAND BAY AND THE GOLF LINKS c1955 C409001
The large building is the Whitsand Bay Hotel; it used to stand at Torpoint on the banks of the Tamar, but was dismantled and re-erected here. Down on the shore is the little village of Portwrinkle, another ex-pilchard fishing village.

CRAFTHOLE, THE VILLAGE c1955 C409008
This view remains largely unchanged, even down to the detail of the roofed porches on the left. On the right is the Crafthole Methodist Chapel, built in 1867, while the house jutting out into the road on the left is now the shop and Post Office.

WHITSAND BAY 1906 55406
Three-quarters of a mile offshore from Whitsand Bay, visible only through the buoy marking her position, is the wreck of the 'James Egan Layne', an American liberty ship which was torpedoed on 21 March 1942. It is probably the most dived-on wreck in Britain - on calm summer days there is usually a large fleet of dive boats anchored at the site.

WHITSAND BAY, THE BEACH 1930 83300

This shows the first of the plague of holiday chalets which swept along the cliffside before planning regulations prevented their building. Today there are hundreds, many of them owned by Plymothians who come out at weekends to enjoy Whitsand Bay's four miles of sand.

WHITSAND BAY AND RAME HEAD c1955 C53035

The small square chapel on Rame Head is that of St Michael, built in the 14th century; it originally housed a beacon to guide ships into Plymouth Sound just round the corner. Eight miles offshore is the Eddystone Lighthouse, the fifth tower to stand on the famous reef and completed in 1882.

CAWSAND, THE SQUARE c1955 C53006
The twin villages of Cawsand and Kingsand nestle into the hills on the west of Cawsand Bay; they were once, like so many Cornish villages, a centre for smugglers.

CAWSAND AND KINGSAND, GENERAL VIEW 1904 52421
The houses in the foreground are in Cawsand, those in the background in Kingsand. At one time the county boundary, now defined by the River Tamar two miles to the north, ran between the two villages, and the old boundary stone can still be seen beside the road.

Index

www.francisfrith.com

The Francis Frith Collection publishes over 100 new titles each year. A selection of those currently available is listed below. For latest catalogue please contact The Francis Frith Collection.

Town Books 96 pages, approximately 75 photos. ***County and Themed Books*** 128 pages, approximately 135 photos (unless specified). Pocket Albums are miniature editions of Frith local history books 128 pages, approximately 95 photos.

Accrington Old and New
Alderley Edge and Wilmslow
Amersham, Chesham and Rickmansworth
Andover
Around Abergavenny
Around Alton
Aylesbury
Barnstaple
Bedford
Bedfordshire
Berkshire Living Memories
Berkshire Pocket Album
Blackpool Pocket Album
Bognor Regis
Bournemouth
Bradford
Bridgend
Bridport
Brighton and Hove
Bristol
Buckinghamshire
Calne Living Memories
Camberley Pocket Album
Canterbury Cathedral
Cardiff Old and New
Chatham and the Medway Towns
Chelmsford
Chepstow Then and Now
Cheshire
Cheshire Living Memories
Chester
Chesterfield
Chigwell
Christchurch
Churches of East Cornwall
Clevedon
Clitheroe
Corby Living Memories
Cornish Coast
Cornwall Living Memories
Cotswold Living Memories
Cotswold Pocket Album
Coulsdon, Chipstead and Woodmansterne
County Durham
Cromer, Sheringham and Holt
Dartmoor Pocket Album
Derby
Derbyshire
Derbyshire Living Memories
Devon
Devon Churches
Dorchester

Dorset Coast Pocket Album
Dorset Living Memories
Dorset Villages
Down the Dart
Down the Severn
Down the Thames
Dunmow, Thaxted and Finchingfield
Durham
East Anglia Pocket Album
East Devon
East Grinstead
Edinburgh
Ely and The Fens
Essex Pocket Album
Essex Second Selection
Essex: The London Boroughs
Exeter
Exmoor
Falmouth
Farnborough, Fleet and Aldershot
Folkestone
Frome
Furness and Cartmel Peninsulas
Glamorgan
Glasgow
Glastonbury
Gloucester
Gloucestershire
Greater Manchester
Guildford
Hailsham
Hampshire
Harrogate
Hastings and Bexhill
Haywards Heath Living Memories
Heads of the Valleys
Heart of Lancashire Pocket Album
Helston
Herefordshire
Horsham
Humberside Pocket Album
Huntingdon, St Neots and St Ives
Hythe, Romney Marsh and Ashford
Ilfracombe
Ipswich Pocket Album
Isle of Wight
Isle of Wight Living Memories
King's Lynn
Kingston upon Thames
Lake District Pocket Album
Lancashire Living Memories
Lancashire Villages

Available from your local bookshop or from the publisher

The Francis Frith Collection Titles (continued)

Lancaster, Morecambe and Heysham Pocket Album
Leeds Pocket Album
Leicester
Leicestershire
Lincolnshire Living Memoires
Lincolnshire Pocket Album
Liverpool and Merseyside
London Pocket Album
Ludlow
Maidenhead
Maidstone
Malmesbury
Manchester Pocket Album
Marlborough
Matlock
Merseyside Living Memories
Nantwich and Crewe
New Forest
Newbury Living Memories
Newquay to St Ives
North Devon Living Memories
North London
North Wales
North Yorkshire
Northamptonshire
Northumberland
Northwich
Nottingham
Nottinghamshire Pocket Album
Oakham
Odiham Then and Now
Oxford Pocket Album
Oxfordshire
Padstow
Pembrokeshire
Penzance
Petersfield Then and Now
Plymouth
Poole and Sandbanks
Preston Pocket Album
Ramsgate Old and New
Reading Pocket Album
Redditch Living Memories
Redhill to Reigate
Richmond
Ringwood
Rochdale
Romford Pocket Album
Salisbury Pocket Album
Scotland
Scottish Castles
Sevenoaks and Tonbridge
Sheffield and South Yorkshire Pocket Album
Shropshire
Somerset
South Devon Coast
South Devon Living Memories
South East London
Southampton Pocket Album
Southend Pocket Album

Southport
Southwold to Aldeburgh
Stourbridge Living Memories
Stratford upon Avon
Stroud
Suffolk
Suffolk Pocket Album
Surrey Living Memories
Sussex
Sutton
Swanage and Purbeck
Swansea Pocket Album
Swindon Living Memories
Taunton
Teignmouth
Tenby and Saundersfoot
Tiverton
Torbay
Truro
Uppingham
Villages of Kent
Villages of Surrey
Villages of Sussex Pocket Album
Wakefield and the Five Towns Living Memories
Warrington
Warwick
Warwickshire Pocket Album
Wellingborough Living Memories
Wells
Welsh Castles
West Midlands Pocket Album
West Wiltshire Towns
West Yorkshire
Weston-super-Mare
Weymouth
Widnes and Runcorn
Wiltshire Churches
Wiltshire Living Memories
Wiltshire Pocket Album
Wimborne
Winchester Pocket Album
Windermere
Windsor
Wirral
Wokingham and Bracknell
Woodbridge
Worcester
Worcestershire
Worcestershire Living Memories
Wyre Forest
York Pocket Album
Yorkshire
Yorkshire Coastal Memories
Yorkshire Dales
Yorkshire Revisited

See Frith books on the internet at www.francisfrith.com

FRITH PRODUCTS & SERVICES

Francis Frith would doubtless be pleased to know that the pioneering publishing venture he started in 1860 still continues today. Over a hundred and forty years later, The Francis Frith Collection continues in the same innovative tradition and is now one of the foremost publishers of vintage photographs in the world. Some of the current activities include:

Interior Decoration

Today Frith's photographs can be seen framed and as giant wall murals in thousands of pubs, restaurants, hotels, banks, retail stores and other public buildings throughout the country. In every case they enhance the unique local atmosphere of the places they depict and provide reminders of gentler days in an increasingly busy and frenetic world.

Product Promotions

Frith products are used by many major companies to promote the sales of their own products or to reinforce their own history and heritage. Frith promotions have been used by Hovis bread, Courage beers, Scots Porage Oats, Colman's mustard, Cadbury's foods, Mellow Birds coffee, Dunhill pipe tobacco, Guinness, and Bulmer's Cider.

Genealogy and Family History

As the interest in family history and roots grows world-wide, more and more people are turning to Frith's photographs of Great Britain for images of the towns, villages and streets where their ancestors lived; and, of course, photographs of the churches and chapels where their ancestors were christened, married and buried are an essential part of every genealogy tree and family album.

Frith Products

All Frith photographs are available Framed or just as Mounted Prints and Posters (size 23 x 16 inches). These may be ordered from the address below. From time to time other products - Address Books, Calendars, Table Mats, etc - are available.

The Internet

Already ninety thousand Frith photographs can be viewed and purchased on the internet through the Frith websites and a myriad of partner sites.

For more detailed information on Frith companies and products, look at this site:

www.francisfrith.com

See the complete list of Frith Books at:
www.francisfrith.com
This web site is regularly updated with the latest list of publications from The Francis Frith Collection. If you wish to buy books relating to another part of the country that your local bookshop does not stock, you may purchase on-line.

For further information, trade, or author enquiries please contact us at the address below:
The Francis Frith Collection, Frith's Barn, Teffont, Salisbury, Wiltshire, England SP3 5QP.
Tel: +44 (0)1722 716 376 Fax: +44 (0)1722 716 881 Email: sales@francisfrith.co.uk

See Frith books on the internet at www.francisfrith.com

FREE PRINT OF YOUR CHOICE

Mounted Print
Overall size 14 x 11 inches (355 x 280mm)

Choose any Frith photograph in this book.
Simply complete the Voucher opposite and return it with your remittance for £3.50 (to cover postage and handling) and we will print the photograph of your choice in SEPIA (size 11 x 8 inches) and supply it in a cream mount with a burgundy rule line (overall size 14 x 11 inches).
Please note: photographs with a reference number starting with a "Z" are not Frith photographs and cannot be supplied under this offer.
Offer valid for delivery to one UK address only.

PLUS: Order additional Mounted Prints at HALF PRICE - £8.50 each (normally £17.00)
If you would like to order more Frith prints from this book, possibly as gifts for friends and family, you can buy them at half price (with no additional postage and handling costs).

PLUS: Have your Mounted Prints framed
For an extra £17.00 per print you can have your mounted print(s) framed in an elegant polished wood and gilt moulding, overall size 16 x 13 inches (no additional postage and handling required).

IMPORTANT!

These special prices are only available if you use this form to order. You must use the ORIGINAL VOUCHER on this page (no copies permitted). We can only despatch to one UK address. This offer cannot be combined with any other offer.

Send completed Voucher form to:
The Francis Frith Collection, Frith's Barn, Teffont, Salisbury, Wiltshire SP3 5QP

CHOOSE A PHOTOGRAPH FROM THIS BOOK

Voucher for *FREE* and *Reduced Price Frith Prints*

Please do not photocopy this voucher. Only the original is valid, so please fill it in, cut it out and return it to us with your order.

Picture ref no	Page no	Qty	Mounted @ £8.50	Framed + £17.00	Total Cost £
		1	Free of charge*	£	£
			£8.50	£	£
			£8.50	£	£
			£8.50	£	£
			£8.50	£	£
			£8.50	£	£

Please allow 28 days for delivery. Offer available to one UK address only

* Post & handling	£3.50
Total Order Cost	£

Title of this book . . . .

I enclose a cheque/postal order for £ . . . .
made payable to 'The Francis Frith Collection'

OR please debit my Mastercard / Visa / Maestro card, details below

Card Number

Issue No (Maestro only)   Valid from (Maestro)

Expires   Signature

Name Mr/Mrs/Ms . . . .
Address . . . .
. . . .
. . . .
. . . . Postcode . . . .
Daytime Tel No . . . .
Email . . . .

ISBN 1-85937-495-6   Valid to 31/12/09

Can you help us with information about any of the Frith photographs in this book?

We are gradually compiling an historical record for each of the photographs in the Frith archive. It is always fascinating to find out the names of the people shown in the pictures, as well as insights into the shops, buildings and other features depicted.

If you recognize anyone in the photographs in this book, or if you have information not already included in the author's caption, do let us know. We would love to hear from you, and will try to publish it in future books or articles.

Our production team

Frith books are produced by a small dedicated team at offices in the converted Grade II listed 18th-century barn at Teffont near Salisbury, illustrated above. Most have worked with The Francis Frith Collection for many years. All have in common one quality: they have a passion for The Francis Frith Collection. The team is constantly expanding, but currently includes:

Paul Baron, Jason Buck, John Buck, Jenny Coles, Heather Crisp, David Davies, Natalie Davis, Louis du Mont, Isobel Hall, Chris Hardwick, Neil Harvey, Julian Hight, Peter Horne, James Kinnear, Karen Kinnear, Tina Leary, Stuart Login, Sue Molloy, Sarah Roberts, Kate Rotondetto, Eliza Sackett, Terence Sackett, Sandra Sampson, Adrian Sanders, Sandra Sanger, Julia Skinner, Lewis Taylor, Will Tunnicliffe, David Turner and Ricky Williams.